MATH ATTACK!

EXPLORING AMAZING ADAPTATIONS WITH MATH

Robyn Hardyman

PowerKiDS press

New York

Published in 2017 by
The Rosen Publishing Group, Inc.
29 East 21st Street, New York, NY 10010

Cataloging-in-Publication Data
Names: Hardyman, Robyn.
Title: Exploring Amazing Adaptations with Math / Robyn Hardyman.
Description: New York : PowerKids Press, 2017. | Series: Math attack: exploring life science with math | Includes index.
Identifiers: ISBN 9781499431131 (pbk.) | ISBN 9781499431155 (library bound) | ISBN 9781499431148 (6 pack)
Subjects: LCSH: Adaptation (Biology)--Juvenile literature. | Competition (Biology)--Juvenile literature. | Animals--Adaptation--Juvenile literature.
Classification: LCC QH546.H349 2017 | DDC 578.4--dc23

Produced for Rosen by Calcium
Editors for Calcium: Sarah Eason and Jennifer Sanderson
Designers for Calcium: Paul Myerscough and Jennie Child
Picture researcher: Rachel Blount

Picture credits: Cover: Shutterstock: Kuttelvaserova Stuchelova r, Johan Swanepoel tl. Inside: Shutterstock: Apple2499 18, Alexandru Axon 20, Sheila Fitzgerald 11, Gilmanshin 16, Eric Isselee 6, Andrea Izzotti 19, 29t, Jack53 24, Johannviloria 5, Branko Jovanovic 9, Robert L Kothenbeutel 10, Ivan Kuzmin 25, Henrik Larsson 21, Peter Leahy 26, Mountainpix 14–15, Jesse Nguyen 4, Andreas R. 22, Reptiles4all 12, Michael Rosskothen 6–7, 28, SIMON SHIM 13, Audrey Snider-Bell 17, Stockphoto Mania 1, Tomatito 14, Marek Velechovsky 8, Worldswildlifewonders 23, Abeselom Zerit 27, 29b.

Manufactured in the United States of America
CPSIA Compliance Information: Batch #BW17PK: For Further Information contact Rosen Publishing, New York, New York at 1-800-237-9932.

CONTENTS

WHAT ARE ADAPTATIONS?

Almost every place on Earth has animals living in it. Animals are amazing. They can live almost anywhere: in great heat or cold, deep in the oceans, and high up on mountains. Animals have developed **adaptations** to help them survive in their **habitats**. Adaptations are features of an animal's body, or of its behavior, that help it survive.

A hummingbird has a long beak to reach its food inside flowers.

Staying Alive

There are about 8.7 million different species, or kinds, of animals in the world. Each one has features that help it find food, avoid being eaten, and find a mate. For example, a polar bear has very thick fur to keep it warm in the freezing Arctic. A mole has strong claws to help it dig tunnels underground. A turtle has a hard shell to protect it from its enemies. Sometimes, an adaptation is not in the animal's physical features, but in its behavior. Over millions of years, a species learns tricks and skills that help it survive.

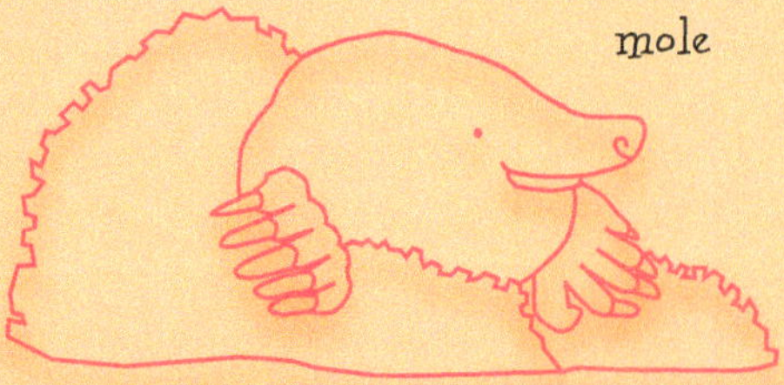

mole

Extreme Adaptations

Some adaptations seem more extreme than others. The puffer fish can puff up its whole body by filling it with water and air, so its enemies cannot swallow it. Other animals, such as chameleons, change color to make themselves invisible.

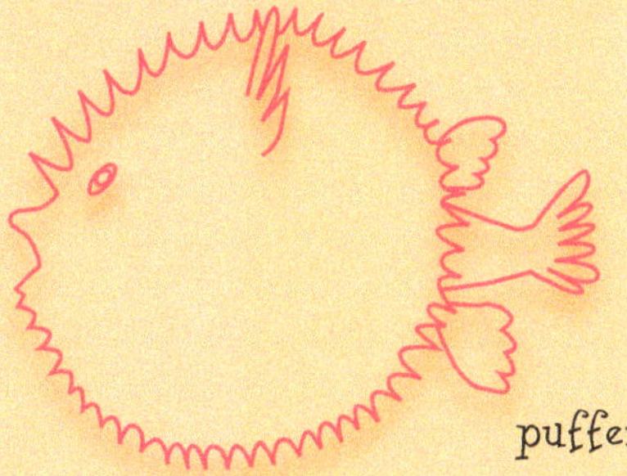

puffer fish

MORE THAN A NUMBER!

BOMBARDIER BEETLES ATTACK THEIR ENEMIES WITH A BOILING MIXTURE OF POISONS. THE MIXTURE EXPLODES WITH A "POP" AS IT IS RELEASED FROM THE BEETLE'S BODY. THE BEETLE DIRECTS THIS JET ACCURATELY. THE JET CAN TRAVEL AS FAR AS 13 FEET (4 M).

The bombardier beetle attacks its enemies with a high-speed stream of poison.

Being Big

Being the biggest animal around can give you a natural advantage over other creatures. It can make you stronger, and scare away **predators**, or animals that might hunt you. Large meat-eaters have bigger brains, too. This helps them plan and carry out attacks on their **prey**.

Giant Bugs

The Hercules beetle is one of the largest bugs in the world. It lives in Central and South America. The males can be up to 7.5 inches (19 cm) long. They are longer than the females because they have huge horns that make up most of their length. They use these to fight each other over the females.

Hercules beetles are so strong, they can carry up to 850 times their own body weight. That is like a person carrying six elephants!

A new-born blue whale drinks about 400 pints (227 l) of its mother's milk every day and gains 8 pounds (4 kg) an hour in weight.

Record Breaker

The biggest animals on Earth are female blue whales. They can be more than 100 feet (30 m) long. Their food, though, is tiny. They eat krill and plankton, which are very small sea creatures. To get enough food they need to eat tons of them every day. They are adapted to have plates fringed with bristles in their mouth. The food is caught in the bristles, then the whale licks it off with its enormous tongue.

MATH ATTACK!

Just the tongue of a female blue whale weighs about 6,000 pounds (2,722 kg). An average person weighs about 200 pounds (91 kg). How many people does it take to weigh the same as one blue whale tongue? Use this calculation to help you solve the problem:

6,000 POUNDS ÷ 200 POUNDS = ? PEOPLE

JUMPING AND RUNNING

Whether they are large or small, animals that can travel far and fast have powerful legs. Some amazing animals, such as kangaroos and wallabies, can move really fast by jumping along!

Before it pounces, the jumping spider spins a line of silk and fixes it to the ground, like a safety rope.

Champion Jumpers

The best jumpers are fleas. These tiny **insects** can jump 220 times their own body length and 150 times their body height. They do not have wings so, instead, they travel by jumping. They store energy in pads on their back legs, then use it to leap upward.

Jumping spiders do not catch their prey in a web: they creep up on it and then pounce. They are smaller than some spiders, but their short legs are powerful. They can jump about 50 times their own body length. That is the same as a person jumping the length of two jumbo jets. These spiders can see well, too. They have four eyes on their face and four more on top of their head.

Running Wild

Some animals run very fast to catch their food, while others run to escape predators. The basilisk lizard can run on water to escape being eaten. It runs at 5.5 miles per hour (9 km/h), fast enough so it does not sink. The fastest land animal is the cheetah. It can reach speeds of up to 54 miles per hour (87 km/h). A cheetah's backbone bends up and down as it runs, so it can take extra-long strides.

MORE THAN A NUMBER!

GRASSHOPPERS ARE AMAZING JUMPERS. THEIR STRONG BACK LEGS ARE LIKE POWERFUL SPRINGS THAT SEND THEM SOARING INTO THE AIR. THEY CAN JUMP 20 TIMES THEIR BODY LENGTH. THAT IS THE EQUIVALENT OF A HUMAN JUMPING THE LENGTH OF A BASKETBALL COURT!

Although grasshoppers are powerful jumpers, they also have wings and can fly.

SPEED

In the animal kingdom, speed can save your life. It can help you escape from your enemies, on fast legs or wings. It can also get you a meal in a high-speed chase. On land, in the air, and in the water, some animals are brilliantly adapted to make them super-speedy.

When a peregrine falcon dives for prey, even birds in mid-flight do not stand a chance of escaping.

Skydiving

The fastest animal in the world is the peregrine falcon. This **bird of prey** hunts birds in mid-flight. When it spots them, it goes into a steep dive at up to 200 miles per hour (320 km/h). This elegant killer has narrow, pointed wings. When it goes into a dive, it tucks the wings into its body and, whoosh, it dive-bombs. It likes to live in high places, such as cliffs and mountains. Some peregrine falcons even live in cities on skyscrapers.

Built for Speed

The sailfish is the fastest fish in the sea. It has a long, pointed nose that gives it a **streamlined** shape. This allows it to move easily through the water. The tall fin on its back looks like the sail of a boat. It helps the sailfish reach speeds of up to 68 miles per hour (110 km/h).

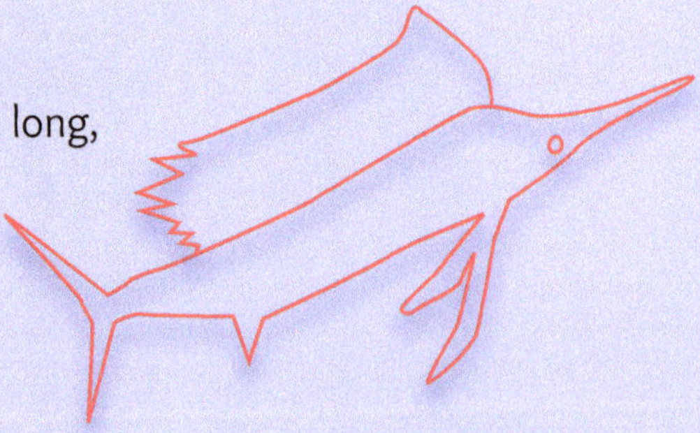

sailfish

Patas monkeys live on the open grasslands of Africa. They are the world's fastest **primates**.

Cheetahs are not the only fast sprinters on land. Male patas monkeys can run away from their predators at speeds of up to 34 miles per hour (55 km/h). They are able do this because they have slender bodies and extra-long legs.

The fastest animal on two legs is the ostrich. It can run at a top speed of 45 miles per hour (72 km/h).

MATH ATTACK!

A cheetah can run at 54 miles per hour (87 km/h). A patas money can run at 34 miles per hour (55 km/h). How much faster is the cheetah than the patas monkey? Use this calculation to help you solve the problem:

54 MILES – 34 MILES = ? MILES

Is There Anybody There?

You can just make out the eyes and feet of this orchid mantis sitting on an orchid. How sneaky is that?

When another animal is out to eat you, if you cannot make a quick getaway it is great to be able to hide. This is called **camouflage**. Animals have evolved some truly fantastic adaptations to camouflage themselves in their habitat.

A Perfect Disguise

The leafy sea dragon is an amazing creature that lives among the seaweed in the ocean. Its body is covered in "pretend seaweed" that makes a perfect disguise. Other animals are adapted for disguise on land. The orchid mantis of Southeast Asia hides not to escape being hunted, but to hunt. This bug is colored the same as the flowers it sits on, waiting for a meal of flies and other small insects to pass by.

In Hiding

Stick-bugs are perfectly hidden, too. Their long, brown bodies look just like the twigs they live on. The bird dung crab spider goes to even greater lengths to hide itself. It tries desperately to look like bird droppings. Its dark brown body is covered with lumps, and it spins threads of white silk that look like the white parts of droppings. It even smells like bird droppings. This is very smart because it attracts small bugs, which the spider eats, but it puts off birds that might want to eat the spider. That is cunning!

MORE THAN A NUMBER!

THERE ARE ABOUT 2,000 DIFFERENT KINDS OF CRAB SPIDERS. THEY LIVE IN ASIA. THEIR TWO LONG PAIRS OF FRONT LEGS LOOK LIKE THE LEGS AND PINCERS OF A CRAB. THEY LIE IN WAIT FOR THEIR PREY, THEN THEY POUNCE.

The bird dung crab spider is perfectly adapted to look like a bird dropping.

I Can See You!

Sometimes, animals need particularly good hearing or eyesight to live successfully in their habitat. In their effort to survive, many animals have developed senses that are far superior to ours.

Beady Eyes

Birds of prey need excellent vision to spot their prey. Eagles can see rabbits from several miles away, for example. However, the eyes of many insects trump this. Flies and other bugs do not just have one eye: they have thousands. These are called **compound eyes** and they are brilliant at seeing movement. They are what you need when your food is on the move. The position of an animal's eyes is important, too. Animals that need to be able to see all around, have eyes on the sides of their head, unlike humans, who can see only straight ahead.

The eyes on either side of the head of this fly are made up of thousands of small eyes combined.

The rattlesnake uses its forked tongue to smell and taste its surroundings.

Sniff It Out

Some creatures do not smell in the same way we do. For example, the rattlesnake's sense of taste and smell are the same. When it detects a scent, it brings out its forked tongue and picks up scent particles from the air. It then brings its tongue in and presses it against the roof of its mouth to identify the scent. Moths do not have noses. They detect smells using their **antennae**. They can smell a female from at least 1 mile (1.6 km) away.

MATH ATTACK!

A dog has a sense of smell 100 times better than a human's. Bears, on the other hand, have a sense of smell 2,200 times better than a human's. They are the best sniffers of any land animal. If a person can smell a sausage from 10 feet (3 m) away, how far away can the sausage be for a dog to be able to smell it, and for a bear to be able to smell it? Use this calculation to help you solve the problems:

10 FEET X 100 TIMES BETTER SENSE OF SMELL = ? FEET

10 FEET X 2,200 TIMES BETTER SENSE OF SMELL = ? FEET

A Deadly Dose

The spines on the back of a lionfish can deliver a venomous sting.

Sometimes, the world of animals is pretty nasty. Many different kinds of animals have adaptations that they use to kill their prey with deadly venom. Some use this technique to defend themselves, too.

Beautiful but Dangerous

In the waters along the east coast of the United States, lionfish lie in wait. They eat many types of fish, and they can harm you, too. They look pretty but they have spines all along their backs. These spines contain a powerful venom. Lionfish sting their prey with these spines and, soon, the victim is unable to move. The blue-ringed octopus is one of the most dangerous animals in the sea, even though it is only 5–8 inches (12–20 cm) long. Its blue rings glow when it is threatened. When it is attacked, it uses its venom to paralyze its attacker. These octopuses have even killed humans.

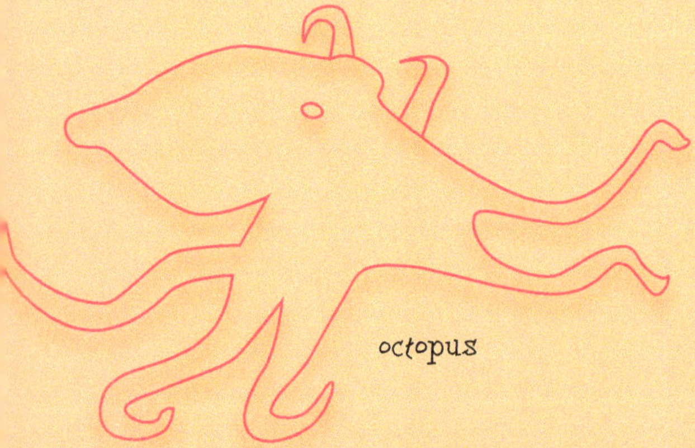

octopus

Danger on Land

The deadly fat-tailed scorpion has developed a powerful sting in a hollow tube on the end of its tail, connected to a bag of venom. It catches a meal in its powerful front claws, then swings its fat tail over to stab it. Snakes are adapted to poison their prey, too. The world's most venomous snake is the inland taipan. One bite contains enough venom to kill dozens of humans.

MORE THAN A NUMBER!

A BRAZILIAN WANDERING SPIDER HOLDS ENOUGH VENOM TO KILL 225 MICE. A BOX JELLYFISH CAN STING A PERSON TO DEATH WITH ITS TENTACLES IN FEWER THAN 5 MINUTES. AMAZINGLY, EACH CONE SNAIL CONTAINS UP TO 100 TYPES OF VENOM.

The venom in the scorpion's sting makes its prey unable to move, so it can be eaten.

ARMED AND DANGEROUS

The Siberian tiger is the world's biggest cat. It sinks its teeth into its prey like daggers.

There are times when animals need as many weapons as they can find to defend themselves from attack or to kill. Animals have adapted to have an impressive array of claws, spikes, teeth, shells, beaks, and more.

Attack!

The terrifying teeth of the big cats are brilliantly designed to deliver a killer bite. The Siberian tiger has long, sharp teeth and a very powerful jaw. The barn owl, in contrast, uses its sharp **talons**, or claws, like a ring of tiny spears to kill a mouse. The mantis shrimp has yet another weapon. Its front claws shoot out at top speed in a blow with the force of a bullet, to stun its prey.

Defense

The defense adaptations of some animals can be very impressive. The bony scales of caimans and crocodiles are like suits of armor, protecting them from attack. On their long back legs, weta bugs have spines, which give painful scratches to any attacker. Their strong jaws also deliver a painful bite. If you are looking for spines, the Texas horned lizard and the thorny devil have plenty, and they know how to use them. So too do hedgehogs and porcupines.

MATH ATTACK!

The cassowary bird cannot fly, but its toes have claws that are 5 inches (13 cm) long. It uses them to tear open its prey. Cassowaries have three toes on each foot. How many claws do they have altogether? What is the combined length of all their claws? Use these calculations to help you solve the problems:

2 FEET X 3 CLAWS = ? CLAWS

? CLAWS X 5 INCHES = ? INCHES

The cassowary can run at speeds of up to 30 miles per hour (48 km/h).

Neat Tricks

The animal kingdom is full of creatures with sneaky adaptations to help them survive. They can change color or shape, grow new parts, or create the most disgusting smells.

Cuttlefish have eight arms and two long tentacles for feeding. They can see both in front of themselves and behind at the same time.

That Is Confusing

The cuttlefish has a cunning and impressive trick. When it is attacked, it squirts out clouds of black ink into the water. Its attacker cannot see and becomes confused, giving the cuttlefish time to escape. Sea cucumbers go to even greater lengths. They squirt their insides out when in danger. Their insides can regrow in a few months.

All Change

Some animals can change color to suit their location. Seahorses, squids, and octopuses can all change color quickly to blend in with their surroundings. Other animals do this more slowly. To match the flowers they sit on, goldenrod crab spiders can change from white to yellow and back. It takes about 30 days for a goldenrod crab spider to change from white to yellow, but just 7 days to change the other way.

MORE THAN A NUMBER!

SOME ANIMALS USE A STINKY TRICK TO STAY SAFE. THE LESSER ANTEATER'S FOUL-SMELLING ODOR IS ABOUT 4 TO 7 TIMES STRONGER THAN THAT OF THE SKUNK. IT IS POSSIBLE TO SMELL THE LESSER ANTEATER UP TO 160 FEET (50 M) AWAY.

This goldenrod spider hiding on a yellow flower has caught a tasty meal.

Do Not Fall!

The woods and forests of the world are full of animals of all kinds: birds, insects, frogs, and **mammals**. Living up in the trees brings the challenge of keeping your balance as it is important not to fall. The animals that cannot fly have met this challenge with some awesome adaptations.

The long fingers of the concolor gibbon grip onto trees like hooks.

Get a Grip

Many kinds of monkeys and apes live in the trees. Monkeys have tails but apes do not. The orangutan is an ape that lives in the forests of Southeast Asia. It has very long and strong arms and legs to help it reach from branch to branch. It also has long fingers to hold on tightly. The concolor gibbon is an even more agile ape. It can zoom through the trees, swinging hand over hand, with its slender body and long limbs.

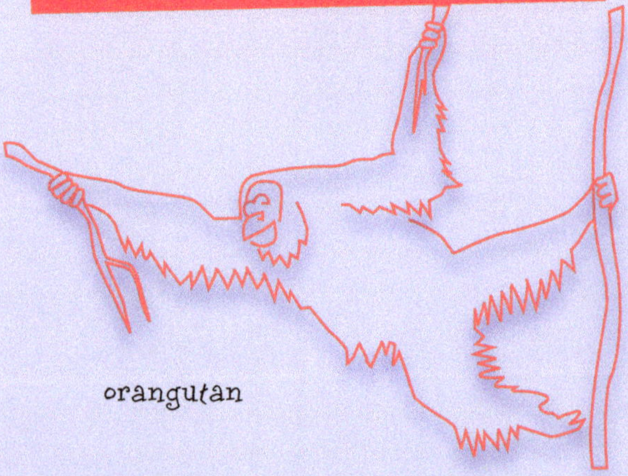

orangutan

Magnificent Tails

Sleeping in trees can be a problem: you do not want to fall off in the night. The colobus monkey has a hard sitting pad on its bottom to help it sleep sitting up. It also has a magnificently long tail. It uses its tail to steer and change direction as it moves through the trees during the day. The spider monkey also has an amazing tail. It works like an extra hand, curling around branches to grip them tight.

The spider monkey hangs on with its tail, leaving its arms free for feeding.

MATH ATTACK!

A troop of 6 spider monkeys is up in the trees, hanging on by their tails. Each monkey has 2 arms, 2 legs, and 1 tail. How many limbs does the group have altogether? Use this calculation to help you solve the problem:

2 ARMS + 2 LEGS + 1 TAIL = ? LIMBS X 6 MONKEYS = ? LIMBS

LIVING IN THE DARK

As the sun sets and many animals are preparing to sleep, a whole new world of animals comes to life. These are the creatures of the night. Some use the darkness to hide from predators; some prefer the cool of the night to the heat of the day. Others are fierce hunters. All of them have adaptations to help them survive in the dark.

Nighttime Hunters

The Cuban boa snake does not see its prey. Instead, it finds it from the heat it gives off. It senses this heat using tiny holes along the bottom of its jaw. The barn owl uses its amazing sense of hearing to find a meal. A barn owl has one ear higher than the other, so it can focus on sounds from above and below. It can tell precisely where a sound is coming from.

The barn owl listens for small mammals, such as mice and voles, then swoops in for the kill.

Seeing in the Dark

Bats have a special trick to find their way in the dark. They send out clicking noises and listen for the echoes as these sounds bounce off the surfaces around them. Other night animals, such as the wood mouse, have huge eyes to catch every bit of light.

Bats catch bugs in their mouth as they fly through the air.

Constant Darkness

Some creatures live where it is always dark. The sun's light never reaches the deepest parts of the ocean. Here live some of the most extraordinary animals, which must find their food and mate in the darkness. The female anglerfish has a long "fishing lure" on its head. This glows in the dark to attract prey.

anglerfish

MORE THAN A NUMBER!

SUNLIGHT CANNOT REACH INTO THE OCEAN BELOW ABOUT 3,300 FEET (1,000 M). ANGLERFISH AND OTHER CREATURES CAN LIVE MORE THAN 6,500 FEET (2,000 M) BELOW THE SURFACE. DOWN THERE, IT IS PITCH BLACK AND VERY COLD.

A Precious World

We have seen how the creatures of the animal kingdom are perfectly adapted to suit their surroundings. Wherever they live, whether it is at the bottom of the deepest ocean or in the tops of rain forest trees, nature has given them the tools they need to survive.

A Rich Diversity

It is this great variety, or diversity, of types of animal that makes the natural world so successful and so precious. It is very important that we make sure we do not harm or destroy habitats, so that animals cannot live there. It is also important that we do not hunt or harm any creature to the point where it dies out, or becomes **extinct**.

Leatherback turtles are now in danger of dying out because people have hunted them and polluted their waters.

The animals that are most in danger of becoming extinct are in that situation because of the things people have done. We have hunted animals for their fur or other parts, or to eat. We have cut down forests, drained wetlands, and **polluted** the ocean. We should admire the wonderful ways in which animals have adapted, and leave them to continue to live successfully in their habitats.

The snow leopard is colored to suit its snowy habitat, and its thick fur keeps it warm.

MATH ATTACK!

Snow leopards live in the snowy mountain areas of China, Pakistan, India, and Nepal. They are hunted for their beautiful fur, and their numbers are falling. There are fewer than 5,000 left in the wild. If there are 5,000 snow leopards alive today, and their numbers are falling by 500 a year, how many snow leopards will be left in 8 years' time? Use this calculation to help you solve the problem:

500 SNOW LEOPARDS X 8 YEARS = ? SNOW LEOPARDS

5,000 SNOW LEOPARDS – ? SNOW LEOPARDS = ? SNOW LEOPARDS REMAINING

ANSWERS

Now that you have read so many facts about animal adaptations, try to learn more about the amazing ways that animals adapt to survive. Here are the answers to the Math Attack problems. How did you score?

PAGE 7:

6,000 POUNDS ÷ 200 POUNDS = 30 PEOPLE

PAGE 11:

54 MILES - 34 MILES = 20 MILES

PAGE 15:

10 FEET X 100 TIMES BETTER SENSE OF SMELL = 1,000 FEET

10 FEET X 2,200 TIMES BETTER SENSE OF SMELL = 22,000 FEET

THAT IS OVER 4 MILES!

PAGE 19:

2 FEET X 3 CLAWS =
6 CLAWS

6 CLAWS X 5 INCHES =
30 INCHES

PAGE 23:

2 ARMS + 2 LEGS + 1 TAIL = 5 LIMBS X
6 MONKEYS = 30 LIMBS

PAGE 27:

500 SNOW LEOPARDS X 8 YEARS =
4,000 SNOW LEOPARDS

5,000 SNOW LEOPARDS –
4,000 SNOW LEOPARDS =
1,000 SNOW
LEOPARDS REMAINING

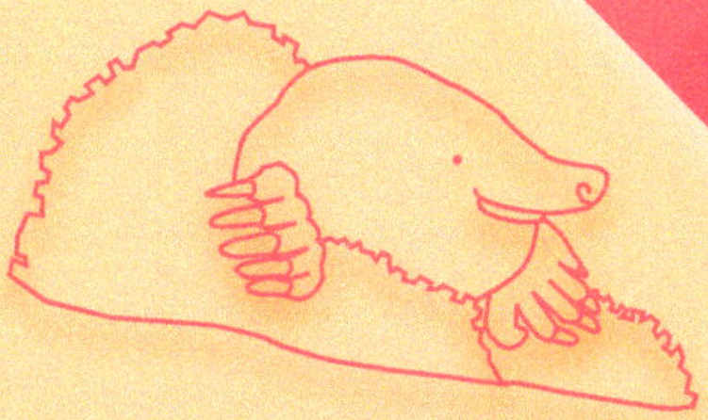

GLOSSARY

adaptations Features of an animal's body, or of its behavior, that help it survive.

antennae Long, thin stalks on an animal's head that are used for sensing.

bird of prey A bird that hunts other animals for food.

camouflage The way an animal blends in with its surroundings.

compound eyes Eyes made up of thousands of smaller eyes.

extinct When there are no more of a type of animal left alive in the world.

habitats Places where an animal or plant lives.

insects Animals that have six legs and bodies divided into three parts: a head, thorax, and abdomen. Some insects have wings attached to the thorax.

mammals Animals that have hair and feed their young with milk.

polluted Filled with harmful substances such as oil, garbage, or poison.

predators Animals that eat other animals.

prey An animal that is eaten by another animal.

primates Mammals with a developed brain, eyes facing forward, a shortened nose, and thumbs that can move forward to touch the other fingers on the same hand.

streamlined A smooth shape that cuts easily through water or air.

talons Claws.

venom A poisonous substance made in the bodies of some animals. It is injected into victims with a bite or sting.

Further Reading

Books

Davies, N. *Extreme Animals: The Toughest Creatures on Earth.* Somerville, MA: Candlewick, 2009.

Mahoney, E. *20 Fun Facts About Amphibian Adaptations.* New York, NY: Gareth Stevens, 2016.

Rajczak, K. *20 Fun Facts About Insect Adaptations.* New York, NY: Gareth Stevens, 2016.

Spelman, L. *National Geographic Animal Encyclopedia.* Washington, DC: National Geographic, 2012.

Websites

Due to the changing nature of Internet links, PowerKids Press has developed an online list of websites related to the subject of this book. This site is updated regularly. Please use this link to access the list:
www.powerkidslinks.com/ma/adapt

INDEX